MIND MUSE

Mindful Meditation

A Beginner's Guide to Cultivating Inner Peace and Well-Being

Dedicated to all those who seek a more peaceful, mindful, and fulfilling life. May this book serve as a guide and inspiration on your journey toward greater self-awareness, compassion, and happiness.

"Embrace the present moment and find peace within. Mindfulness and Meditation, the keys to a fulfilling life."

Mind Muse

Contents

Foreword

The practice of mindfulness and meditation has been around for thousands of years, but in recent decades, it has gained renewed attention and popularity as a powerful tool for enhancing physical, mental, and emotional health. With the increasing demands and stresses of modern life, it is more important than ever to find ways to cultivate inner peace, focus, and resilience.

This book offers a comprehensive and accessible guide to the art and science of mindfulness and meditation, suitable for both beginners and experienced practitioners. It explores the definition of mindfulness, its benefits, and the various techniques and practices that can help you incorporate mindfulness and meditation into your daily life.

The author provides clear and practical instructions, helpful tips, and inspiring insights to support your journey towards greater awareness, compassion, and well-being. Whether you are looking to reduce stress and anxiety, improve focus and productivity, deepen your relationships, or simply live a more meaningful and fulfilling life, this book has something for everyone.

We hope this book will be an indispensable resource for you

on your path to mindfulness and meditation, and we trust that it will offer you the guidance, inspiration, and motivation you need to embark on this journey with confidence.

So, let us begin!

Preface

"This book is an exploration of mindfulness and meditation, two practices that have the power to transform our lives. When I first encountered mindfulness and meditation, I was skeptical. I had always thought of them as "woo-woo" or "new-age" concepts that were of little practical use in the real world. But as I delved deeper into the science behind these practices, I began to see the incredible potential they held.

Over the years, I've had the privilege of studying with some of the world's leading mindfulness and meditation experts, and I've been struck by how many people's lives have been transformed by these practices. From reducing stress and anxiety to improving focus and productivity, the benefits of mindfulness and meditation are simply too good to ignore.

This book is for anyone who is curious about mindfulness and meditation but doesn't know where to start. Whether you're a complete beginner or have been practicing for years, you'll find something in these pages that will help deepen your practice and bring more peace, joy, and purpose into your life. I hope that by reading this book, you'll gain a new appreciation for the power of mindfulness and meditation, and will be inspired to integrate these practices into your own life."

Acknowledgement

"I would like to express my deep gratitude to all those who have supported and encouraged me throughout the writing of this book. I am especially grateful to my family, who has always been my source of inspiration and love. I also want to extend my heartfelt thanks to my friends and colleagues, who have provided me with invaluable insights, encouragement, and support.

I would also like to thank my editor and publisher, who believed in me and helped me turn my ideas into reality. This book would not have been possible without their expert guidance and support.

Finally, I would like to acknowledge all those who have dedicated their lives to the study and practice of mindfulness and meditation. It is their tireless work and research that has made it possible for us to better understand the power and potential of these ancient practices.

This book is dedicated to all of you."

I. Introduction

Welcome to the world of mindfulness and meditation! In this book, you will learn how to cultivate a daily mindfulness practice that will help you reduce stress, improve your health, and increase your happiness. Whether you are a complete beginner or you've been practicing mindfulness for a while, this book is designed to provide you with the tools and guidance you need to deepen your practice and experience its many benefits.

Mindfulness and meditation are ancient practices that have been used for centuries to promote inner peace, well-being, and spiritual growth. In recent years, mindfulness and meditation have gained widespread popularity and recognition as powerful tools for improving mental and physical health. Scientific research has shown that regular mindfulness and meditation practice can help reduce stress, improve sleep, boost the immune system, reduce symptoms of anxiety and depression, and increase happiness and overall life satisfaction.

In this book, we will explore the many benefits of mindfulness and meditation, and we will provide you with practical tools and techniques that you can use to start your own mindfulness and meditation practice. We will begin by exploring what mindfulness is and why it is so important, and we will introduce you to simple mindfulness techniques that you can incorporate into your daily routine. We will then delve into the world of meditation, including different types of meditation, how to create a daily meditation practice, and how to use meditation to deepen your mindfulness practice.

Throughout this book, we will provide you with tips, tricks, and guidance to help you overcome common obstacles and maintain a consistent mindfulness and meditation practice. We will also explore mindfulness and meditation in daily life, including how to incorporate mindfulness into your eating and drinking habits, your exercise routine, and your relationships with others. And finally, we will explore advanced mindfulness and meditation techniques, including mindful breathing, loving-kindness meditation, chakra meditation, and mantra meditation.

By the end of this book, you will have a deep understanding of the power of mindfulness and meditation, and you will have the tools you need to cultivate a successful mindfulness and meditation practice. Whether you are looking to reduce stress, improve your health, or increase your happiness, this book will provide you with the guidance and support you need to start your journey toward greater peace, joy, and fulfillment.

So, let's get started! In this first chapter, we will explore what mindfulness is and why it is so important. By the end of this chapter, you will have a clear understanding of what mindfulness is, why it is so valuable, and how it can improve your life in countless ways. So, let's begin our journey towards mindfulness, meditation, and a happier, healthier, and more fulfilling life.

A. Purpose of the Book

The purpose of this book is to provide you with a comprehensive guide to mindfulness and meditation and to help you cultivate a successful mindfulness and meditation practice. This book is designed for people of all levels of experience, from complete beginners to those who have been practicing mindfulness and meditation for a while. Whether you are looking to reduce stress, improve your health, or increase your happiness, this book will provide you with the tools and guidance you need to start and maintain a successful mindfulness and meditation practice.

In today's fast-paced world, it can be difficult to find peace and contentment. We are constantly bombarded by distractions, and our minds are often filled with worries and fears. This can leave us feeling overwhelmed, stressed, and anxious. But there is hope. Mindfulness and meditation are two powerful tools that can help us find peace, happiness, and well-being, even in the midst of chaos.

Mindfulness is the practice of bringing our attention to the present moment and observing our thoughts, feelings, and sensations without judgment. By practicing mindfulness, we can learn to become more aware of our thoughts and feelings and develop a greater sense of clarity and peace. This can help us to reduce stress and anxiety and to cultivate greater happiness and well-being.

Meditation, on the other hand, is the practice of training our minds to focus and calm our thoughts. Through meditation, we can develop greater mental clarity, increase our emotional stability, and deepen our mindfulness practice. Meditation has been shown to have a wide range of benefits, including reducing stress and anxiety, improving sleep, boosting the immune system, and increasing happiness and overall life satisfaction.

This book will guide you through the process of starting and maintaining a mindfulness and meditation practice. We will begin by exploring what mindfulness and meditation are and why they are so important. We will then delve into the world of mindfulness, introducing you to simple mindfulness techniques that you can incorporate into your daily routine. We will also explore the benefits of mindfulness and how to overcome common obstacles to practicing mindfulness.

Next, we will turn our attention to meditation, exploring different types of meditation, including mindfulness meditation, loving-kindness meditation, chakra meditation, and mantra meditation. We will provide you with practical tips and guidance for starting your own meditation practice, and for deepening your meditation practice over time. We will also explore how to use meditation to enhance your mindfulness practice.

Finally, we will explore mindfulness and meditation in daily life, including how to incorporate mindfulness into your eating and drinking habits, your exercise routine, and your relationships with others. We will also provide you with advanced mindfulness and meditation techniques that you can use to deepen your practice and achieve your goals.

By the end of this book, you will have a deep understanding of the power of mindfulness and meditation, and you will have the tools you need to cultivate a successful mindfulness and meditation practice. Whether you are looking to reduce stress, improve your health, or increase your happiness, this book is designed to provide you with the information and support you need to achieve your goals. So, if you are ready to start your journey towards mindfulness, meditation, and a happier, healthier, and more fulfilling life, then this book is for you!

B. Overview of Mindfulness and Meditation

Mindfulness and meditation are two complementary practices that have gained popularity in recent years due to their numerous benefits for physical and mental well-being. Mindfulness is the practice of bringing one's attention to the present moment and observing one's thoughts, feelings, and sensations without judgment. Meditation, on the other hand, is the practice of training the mind to focus and calm one's thoughts. Both practices are rooted in Buddhist teachings but have been adapted for a modern, secular audience.

Mindfulness has been shown to have a wide range of benefits, including reducing stress and anxiety, improving sleep, boosting the immune system, and increasing happiness and overall life satisfaction. It can also help individuals become more aware of their thoughts and feelings, and to develop a greater sense of clarity and peace. Practicing mindfulness on a regular basis can lead to a more mindful and present-oriented life, and can help individuals cultivate a greater sense of well-being.

Meditation, too, has a long list of benefits. It can help to reduce stress and anxiety, improve sleep, boost the immune system, increase happiness and overall life satisfaction, and enhance one's mindfulness practice. There are many different types of meditation, including mindfulness meditation, loving-kindness meditation, chakra meditation, and mantra meditation. Each type of meditation has its own unique focus and techniques, but they all have the goal of training the mind to focus and calm one's thoughts.

In order to get the most out of mindfulness and meditation, it is important to have consistent and regular practice. This can involve setting aside time each day to meditate, or incorporating mindfulness into your daily routines. It is also important to have patience and persistence, as mindfulness and meditation can be challenging practices to master. However, with time and practice, they can become powerful tools for personal growth and well-being.

In this book, we will explore both mindfulness and meditation in depth, providing you with practical tips and guidance for starting and maintaining a successful practice. We will also explore the benefits of each practice and how they can work together to enhance your overall well-being. Whether you are a complete beginner or have been practicing mindfulness and meditation for a while, this book will provide you with the information and support you need to deepen your practice and achieve your goals.

II. What is Mindfulness and Why is it Important?

Mindfulness is the practice of bringing one's attention to the present moment and observing one's thoughts, feelings, and sensations without judgment. It is a simple yet powerful technique that can help individuals cultivate greater awareness, clarity, and peace in their lives. Mindfulness is a skill that can be learned and developed through regular practice, and it has been shown to have a wide range of benefits for both physical and mental well-being.

The practice of mindfulness is rooted in Buddhist teachings but has been adapted for a modern, secular audience. In its simplest form, mindfulness involves paying attention to the present moment and taking notice of your thoughts, feelings, and sensations without judgment. This can involve focusing on your breathing, observing your thoughts as they arise, or simply being aware of the sensations in your body. By practicing mindfulness, you can learn to quiet your mind and become more present, which can help you develop a greater sense of peace and well-being.

One of the key benefits of mindfulness is its ability to reduce stress and anxiety. By becoming more aware of your thoughts and feelings, you can learn to let go of negative and stressful thoughts, and to respond to difficult situations with greater calm and clarity. Mindfulness has also been shown to improve sleep, boost the immune system, and increase happiness and overall life satisfaction.

In addition to its physical and mental health benefits, mindfulness can also help individuals develop greater self-awareness and empathy. By paying close attention to your thoughts and feelings, you can gain a deeper understanding of yourself and others, and develop a greater capacity for compassion and empathy.

Finally, mindfulness can be a valuable tool for personal growth and transformation. By practicing mindfulness, you can learn to quiet your mind, become more present, and develop a greater sense of self-awareness and inner peace. This can help you achieve greater clarity and focus, and can support you in your personal and professional goals.

In this book, we will explore mindfulness in greater detail, providing you with practical tips and guidance for starting and maintaining a successful mindfulness practice. Whether you are new to mindfulness or have been practicing for a while, this section will provide you with the information and support you need to deepen your understanding of this powerful tool for personal growth and well-being.

A. Definition of Mindfulness

Mindfulness can be defined as a mental state achieved by focusing one's awareness on the present moment, while calmly acknowledging and accepting one's feelings, thoughts, and bodily sensations. It is a way of paying attention to the present moment in a non-judgmental and curious manner, with the aim of fostering greater awareness and clarity.

Mindfulness is not simply about paying attention to the present moment, but also involves a conscious effort to cultivate a particular attitude toward one's experiences. This includes a sense of curiosity, openness, and non-judgment. This means that, when practicing mindfulness, one should approach their thoughts and feelings without trying to change them, judge them, or make them go away. Instead, one should simply observe them with an attitude of curiosity and acceptance.

One of the key principles of mindfulness is that it should be practiced in the present moment, without dwelling on the past or worrying about the future. This helps to cultivate a greater sense of focus and awareness and can help reduce stress and anxiety by shifting the mind away from negative and unhelpful thoughts.

Mindfulness can be practiced in a variety of ways, including formal meditation practices, such as mindful breathing, body scan meditation, and loving-kindness meditation, as well as more informal practices, such as mindful walking, eating, and even brushing your teeth. The goal of all mindfulness practices is to cultivate a greater sense of awareness, focus, and inner peace, which can lead to a wide range of physical and mental health benefits.

In this book, we will explore mindfulness in greater detail, including its definition, history, and benefits. We will also provide practical tips and guidance for starting and maintaining a successful mindfulness practice so that you can experience the benefits of mindfulness for yourself. Whether you are new to mindfulness or have been practicing for a while, this section will help you deepen your understanding of this powerful tool for personal growth

B. The Science of Mindfulness

In recent years, mindfulness has gained increasing attention from the scientific community, with a growing body of research exploring its potential benefits for physical and mental health. From reducing stress and anxiety to improving sleep, mood, and cognitive function, the science of mindfulness has shown that this ancient practice can have a profound impact on our well-being.

One of the key ways in which mindfulness benefits our health is by altering the way our brains respond to stress. Research has shown that mindfulness can activate the relaxation response, which is a state of deep rest that slows down the heart rate and lowers blood pressure. This can help to reduce feelings of stress and anxiety and improve our overall mood.

In addition, mindfulness has been shown to have a positive impact on our immune system, helping to boost our natural defense against illness. This is believed to be due to the fact that mindfulness can help to reduce inflammation in the body, which is a key factor in many chronic diseases.

Mindfulness has also been shown to have a positive impact on cognitive function, improving our ability to focus, concentrate, and retain information. This is believed to be due to the way in which mindfulness helps to reduce distractions and calm the mind, allowing us to be more present and engaged in the task at hand.

The benefits of mindfulness are not limited to physical and mental health, however. Research has also shown that mindfulness can have a positive impact on our relationships, by helping us to cultivate greater empathy, compassion, and emotional intelligence. This can help us to build stronger, more fulfilling relationships with the people around us, and can even improve our overall sense of happiness and well-being.

In this section, we will explore the science of mindfulness in greater detail, including the latest research on its benefits and mechanisms of action. Whether you are interested in the scientific basis of mindfulness, or simply want to know more about its potential impact on your health and happiness, this section will provide you with the information you need to make an informed decision.

C. The Benefits of Mindfulness

One of the reasons mindfulness has gained such popularity in recent years is due to the many benefits it can provide. From improving physical and mental health to enhancing personal and professional relationships, mindfulness has the potential to have a profound impact on our lives. Some of the key benefits of mindfulness include:

1. Reduces stress and anxiety: Mindfulness has been shown to be an effective tool for reducing feelings of stress and anxiety. By shifting the focus away from negative thoughts and feelings, and towards the present moment, mindfulness can help to calm the mind and reduce the physical symptoms of stress, such as increased heart rate and blood pressure.

2. Improves physical health: In addition to reducing stress and anxiety, mindfulness has been shown to have a number of positive effects on physical health, including boosting the immune system, reducing inflammation, and improv-

ing sleep.

3. Enhances cognitive function: Mindfulness has been shown to improve cognitive function, including attention, memory, and learning. This is believed to be due to the way in which mindfulness helps to calm the mind and reduce distractions, allowing us to be more present and focused in the task at hand.

4. Improves emotional well-being: Mindfulness has been shown to improve mood and emotional well-being, helping to reduce feelings of depression and anxiety, and fostering a greater sense of happiness and inner peace.

5. Strengthens relationships: By cultivating greater empathy, compassion, and emotional intelligence, mindfulness can help to improve relationships with others. This can lead to greater understanding and connection, and can even help to resolve conflicts.

6. Increases creativity and innovation: By fostering a greater sense of focus and awareness, mindfulness can help to increase creativity and innovation. This can be especially beneficial in professional settings, where fresh ideas and new perspectives are often needed to solve complex problems.

In this section, we will explore each of these benefits in greater detail, providing practical tips and guidance for how you can experience the benefits of mindfulness for yourself. Whether you are looking to improve your physical or mental health, or simply want to enhance your personal and professional relationships, this section will provide you with the information and inspiration you need to get started.

III. Getting Started with Mindfulness

Getting started with mindfulness is easier than you might think, and the benefits can be life-changing. Whether you are new to mindfulness or are looking to expand your existing practice, this section will provide you with the information and guidance you need to get started.

A. Understanding the Basics

The first step in getting started with mindfulness is to understand the basics. This includes learning about the principles of mindfulness and how it can be used to improve your well-being. You will also learn about the different types of mindfulness practices, including mindfulness meditation, mindful breathing, and mindful movement, and how you can choose the right practices for your needs.

B. Setting Your Intentions

Once you have a basic understanding of mindfulness, the next step is to set your intentions. This means taking some time to reflect on why you want to start a mindfulness practice, and what you hope to achieve. This will help you stay motivated and focused as you begin your practice, and will provide you with a sense of purpose as you progress.

C. Creating a Daily Practice

The key to making mindfulness a part of your daily life is to create a consistent practice. This can involve setting aside a specific time each day for mindfulness meditation or incorporating mindful moments into your daily routine. You may also find it helpful to establish a regular routine, such as starting each day with mindful meditation or ending each day with a few minutes of mindful breathing.

D. Incorporating Mindfulness into Your Life

Incorporating mindfulness into your life involves more than just setting aside time for meditation or other mindfulness practices. It also involves being mindful in your daily interactions with others, and in the way you approach tasks and challenges. By incorporating mindfulness into all areas of your life, you will be better able to maintain a consistent practice, and experience the full benefits of mindfulness.

In this section, we will explore each of these steps in greater detail, and provide you with practical tips and guidance for getting started with your own mindfulness practice. Whether you are a busy professional looking to reduce stress and improve your focus, or a stay-at-home parent seeking more peace and happiness, this section will help you get started on your mindfulness journey.

A. Simple Mindfulness Techniques for Beginners

⚜

If you are new to mindfulness, you may be wondering where to start. The good news is that there are many simple mindfulness techniques that you can start using right away to begin experiencing the benefits of mindfulness. In this section, we will explore some of the most effective and accessible mindfulness techniques for beginners.

1. Mindful Breathing

Mindful breathing is one of the simplest and most effective mindfulness techniques and is a great place to start for beginners. To practice mindful breathing, simply find a quiet place to sit, and focus your attention on your breath. Pay attention to the sensation of air moving in and out of your body, and notice any thoughts or emotions that arise. When your mind wanders, simply redirect your focus back to your breath.

1. Body Scan Meditation

The body scan meditation is another great mindfulness technique for beginners. To practice this meditation, simply lie down or sit comfortably, and scan your body from head to toe, noticing any sensations or tension you may be holding. You can also practice this meditation while walking or standing, focusing on different parts of your body as you move.

1. Loving Kindness Meditation

The loving-kindness meditation is a form of mindfulness meditation that involves sending feelings of love and compassion to yourself and others. To practice this meditation, simply find a quiet place to sit, and focus on sending loving kindness to yourself, a loved one, a neutral person, and eventually, to all beings.

These are just a few of the many simple mindfulness techniques that you can start using right away. As you become more familiar with mindfulness and meditation, you can explore more advanced techniques, such as mindfulness of thoughts, or loving-kindness and compassion meditation. The important thing is to start where you are and to be patient and persistent in your practice. With time and effort, you will see the benefits of mindfulness and meditation become more and more evident in your life.

B. Using Mindfulness to Improve Focus and Productivity

One of the many benefits of mindfulness is that it can help to improve focus and productivity. When we are mindful, we are able to focus our attention on the present moment, which helps us to be more engaged and productive in our work.

Here are some ways to use mindfulness to improve focus and productivity:

1. Mindful Breaks

Taking short mindful breaks throughout the day can help to refresh your mind and increase your focus and productivity. To take a mindful break, simply stop what you're doing, and spend a few minutes focusing on your breath, or engaging in a simple mindfulness exercise, such as a body scan or loving-kindness meditation.

1. Mindful Listening

Mindful listening is a form of mindfulness that involves paying full attention to the person who is speaking, without getting distracted by your own thoughts or emotions. When you practice mindful listening in your work or personal life, you are able to communicate more effectively and build stronger relationships with others.

1. Mindful Time Management

Mindful time management is about being intentional and mindful about how you use your time and focusing on the tasks that are most important to you. To practice mindful time management, try to be mindful of how you spend your time throughout the day and set aside specific blocks of time for different tasks and activities.

By incorporating mindfulness into your work and daily routine, you can experience the benefits of increased focus and productivity. With practice, you'll find that you are able to stay more focused, get more done, and be more effective in all areas of your life.

C. Overcoming Obstacles to a Successful Mindfulness Practice

While mindfulness can be incredibly beneficial, it's not always easy to establish a regular practice. Here are some common obstacles that people face, and tips for overcoming them:

1. Lack of Time

One of the most common obstacles to establishing a mindfulness practice is simply not having enough time. However, even a few minutes of mindfulness practice each day can be incredibly beneficial. Try to set aside just a few minutes each day for mindfulness, and gradually increase the amount of time as you become more comfortable with the practice.

1. Difficulty Staying Focused

Another common obstacle to mindfulness is difficulty staying focused. When we first start practicing mindfulness, it can be hard to stay focused on the present moment, as our minds are used to constantly thinking and wandering. To overcome this obstacle, try to be patient with yourself and understand that it takes time to develop this skill. Start with short periods of mindfulness, and gradually increase the length of your practice as you become more comfortable with it.

1. Negative Thoughts and Emotions

Practicing mindfulness can sometimes bring up negative thoughts and emotions that we might have been avoiding. This can be difficult, but it's important to remember that mindfulness is not about avoiding these feelings, but rather about becoming more aware of them and learning to deal with them in a healthy and productive way. Try to be gentle with yourself, and focus on the breath or other mindfulness techniques when negative thoughts arise.

By overcoming these obstacles and developing a regular mindfulness practice, you can experience the many benefits of mindfulness, including reduced stress and anxiety, improved focus and productivity, and a greater sense of peace and well-being.

IV. Meditation for Beginners

Meditation is a powerful tool for promoting mindfulness, reducing stress and anxiety, and improving overall well-being. However, it can be difficult to know where to start. Here are some tips for starting a meditation practice:

A. Find a quiet, comfortable place to sit

The first step in starting a meditation practice is to find a quiet, comfortable place to sit. This could be a chair, cushion, or bench, but the most important thing is that you are comfortable and able to sit still for a period of time.

B. Set a timer

To get started with meditation, it's helpful to set a timer for a specific amount of time. Start with just a few minutes and gradually increase the amount of time as you become more comfortable with the practice.

C. Focus on the breath

One of the simplest ways to start a meditation practice is to focus on the breath. Simply close your eyes and bring your attention to the sensation of the breath moving in and out of the body. Try to focus your attention on the breath, and notice when your mind starts to wander. When this happens, simply bring your attention back to the breath.

D. Don't get discouraged

It's normal for the mind to wander when we first start meditating, and it can be discouraging when this happens. However, it's important to remember that this is part of the process and not to get discouraged. Simply bring your attention back to the breath and continue the practice.

By starting a regular meditation practice and focusing on the breath, you can begin to experience the many benefits of meditation, including reduced stress and anxiety, improved focus and clarity, and a greater sense of inner peace and well-being.

A. Types of Meditation

There are many different types of meditation, each with its own unique approach and benefits. Here are some of the most popular types of meditation:

1.Mindfulness Meditation

Mindfulness meditation is the practice of bringing your attention to the present moment and being fully present in the experience. This type of meditation can help to reduce stress, increase focus and clarity, and improve overall well-being.

2.Loving-Kindness Meditation

Loving-kindness meditation is a type of meditation that involves focusing on feelings of love and compassion for yourself and others. This type of meditation can help to increase feelings of happiness, compassion, and empathy.

3.Body Scan Meditation

Body scan meditation involves lying down or sitting comfortably and focusing your attention on different parts of the body. This type of meditation can help to reduce stress, improve sleep, and increase feelings of relaxation.

4.Movement Meditation

Movement meditation involves slow, deliberate movements that are performed in a mindful and focused manner. This type of meditation can help to increase focus and mindfulness, reduce stress and anxiety, and improve physical health.

5.Mantra Meditation

Mantra meditation involves repeating a specific word or phrase, either silently or out loud, in order to bring the mind into a state of stillness and focus. This type of meditation can help to reduce stress, improve focus and clarity, and increase feelings of peace and well-being.

These are just a few examples of the many different types of meditation. By exploring different types of meditation, you can find the one that is right for you and start experiencing the many benefits of a regular meditation practice.

B. Creating a Daily Meditation Practice

One of the keys to a successful meditation practice is to make it a part of your daily routine. Here are some tips for creating a daily meditation practice:

1.Set a Schedule

The first step in creating a daily meditation practice is to set a schedule for your meditation sessions. It's important to choose a time of day that works well for you, whether it's first thing in the morning, during a lunch break, or just before bed. Try to stick to this schedule as much as possible, and make it a non-negotiable part of your daily routine.

2.Start Small

When you're first getting started with meditation, it can be helpful to start with short, 5-10 minute sessions. As you become more comfortable with the practice, you can gradually increase the length of your meditation sessions.

3.Find a Comfortable and Quiet Space

It's important to find a quiet and comfortable space for your meditation practice. This could be a dedicated meditation room, a quiet corner of your home, or even a quiet outdoor space. Make sure that your meditation space is free from distractions, and that it feels peaceful and calming.

4.Use Guided Meditations

If you're just getting started with meditation, it can be helpful to use guided meditations to help you stay focused and on track. There are many resources available for guided meditations, including audio and video meditations, guided meditation apps, and online meditation classes.

5.Stay Committed

Creating a daily meditation practice takes time and commitment. It's important to stick with it, even on days when it feels difficult or when you're feeling particularly stressed or busy. Remember that the benefits of meditation will only become apparent over time, and that consistency is key.

By following these tips, you can create a daily meditation practice that works well for you, and start reaping the many benefits of mindfulness and meditation.

C. Using Meditation to Deepen Your Mindfulness Practice

Meditation and mindfulness are closely related, and practicing meditation can be an effective way to deepen your mindfulness practice. Here's how you can use meditation to enhance your mindfulness:

1. Focus on the Present Moment

One of the core principles of mindfulness is being present in the moment. During meditation, you can focus on your breath, your body sensations, or a mantra or visualization to help you stay present. This focus on the present moment can help you cultivate mindfulness in your everyday life.

2. Develop Self-Awareness

Meditation can help you develop self-awareness by giving you time to reflect on your thoughts and emotions. By observing your thoughts and emotions without judgment, you can gain a deeper understanding of yourself, and learn to manage your reactions to stress and negativity.

3. Cultivate Compassion and Kindness

Meditation can also help you cultivate compassion and kindness. There are many different types of meditation that focus on these qualities, including loving-kindness meditation, which involves sending positive thoughts and feelings to yourself and others.

4. Enhance Physical and Mental Well-Being

Meditation has been shown to have a positive impact on physical and mental well-being. Regular meditation can help reduce stress and anxiety, improve sleep, increase focus and concentration, and enhance overall well-being.

By using meditation to deepen your mindfulness practice, you can tap into the many benefits of mindfulness and meditation, and become a happier, healthier, and more mindful person.

D. The Benefits of Meditation

Meditation is a powerful tool for improving physical and mental well-being and has been shown to have a number of benefits, including:

1. Reduces Stress and Anxiety

One of the most well-known benefits of meditation is its ability to reduce stress and anxiety. By calming the mind and reducing the body's stress response, meditation can help you manage stress and anxiety more effectively, and feel more relaxed and at peace.

2. Improves Sleep

Meditation can also help improve sleep. By calming the mind and reducing stress and anxiety, meditation can help you fall asleep more easily and sleep more deeply, leaving you feeling refreshed and rejuvenated in the morning.

3. Increases Focus and Concentration

Meditation can help improve focus and concentration, making it easier to stay focused and productive throughout the day. This can be especially helpful for people who struggle with distractions and are easily distracted.

4. Boosts the Immune System

Studies have shown that meditation can have a positive impact on the immune system, helping to boost immunity and reduce the risk of illness.

5. Enhances Emotional Well-being

Meditation can also help enhance emotional well-being by reducing negative emotions, such as anger and frustration, and increasing positive emotions, such as happiness and content-ment.

These are just a few of the many benefits of meditation. By incorporating meditation into your daily routine, you can tap into these benefits, and feel happier, healthier, and more focused.

V. Mindfulness and Meditation in Daily Life

While mindfulness and meditation are often associated with quiet, solitary activities, they can be integrated into daily life in many different ways. Here are a few tips for making mindfulness and meditation a part of your daily routine:

1. Practice Mindfulness Throughout the Day

One of the easiest ways to incorporate mindfulness into your daily life is to practice it throughout the day. This could involve taking a few deep breaths when you feel stressed, paying attention to your breath while you wait in line, or simply noticing and appreciating the sensations in your body as you move throughout your day.

2. Make Time for Meditation

While mindfulness can be practiced throughout the day, it's also important to set aside time for formal meditation practice. This could involve sitting quietly for a few minutes each day, or engaging in a longer, more structured meditation practice.

3. Use Guided Meditations

For those who are new to meditation, guided meditation can be a helpful way to get started. There are many free apps and websites that offer guided meditations, which can help you relax and focus, and deepen your meditation practice over time.

4. Create a Calm Environment

Creating a calm and supportive environment for your meditation practice can help you get the most out of it. This might involve finding a quiet place to meditate, or lighting candles and burning incense to create a peaceful atmosphere.

5. Make it a Habit

Finally, making mindfulness and meditation a habit is key to making them a part of your daily life. Try to practice mindfulness and meditation at the same time each day, and make them a non-negotiable part of your routine. With time, they will become as natural and automatic as brushing your teeth or eating breakfast.

By incorporating mindfulness and meditation into your daily life, you can experience their many benefits, and enjoy a greater sense of peace, focus, and well-being.

A. Incorporating Mindfulness and Meditation into Your Routine

Making mindfulness and meditation a part of your daily routine requires some planning and effort, but the benefits are well worth it. Here are some tips for incorporating these practices into your routine:

1. Set a Schedule

Setting a schedule for your mindfulness and meditation practice is a great way to make it a habit. Choose a time that works for you, and make sure to stick to it every day. Whether you choose to meditate in the morning, at lunchtime, or before bed, having a set schedule will help you remember to practice and make it a non-negotiable part of your day.

2. Find a Comfortable and Quiet Place

Having a quiet and comfortable place to meditate is key to making your mindfulness and meditation practice successful. Find a space where you can sit comfortably and not be disturbed, and make sure that it is free of distractions. This could be a room in your home, a quiet park, or even your car if it's a place where you feel calm and peaceful.

3. Start Small

It can be overwhelming to try to meditate for an hour right away, so start small. Aim to meditate for 5-10 minutes a day, and gradually increase the time as you become more comfortable with the practice.

4. Use Guided Meditations

For those who are new to meditation, guided meditation can be a helpful way to get started. There are many free apps and websites that offer guided meditations, which can help you relax and focus, and deepen your meditation practice over time.

5. Make it a Priority

Finally, it's important to make mindfulness and meditation a priority. Treat your practice like any other important appointment, and make sure to set aside the time and space you need to make it a regular part of your life.

By following these tips and making mindfulness and meditation a priority, you can experience the many benefits of these practices and make them a regular part of your routine.

B. Mindful Eating and Drinking

Eating and drinking are some of the most basic and important activities we engage in, yet they are often done mindlessly. Mindful eating and drinking, on the other hand, is a way to focus your attention on the present moment and bring greater awareness and intention to these activities. Here's how you can incorporate mindfulness into your eating and drinking:

1. Slow Down

One of the biggest benefits of mindful eating is that it helps you slow down and enjoy your food. Take the time to savor each bite, and pay attention to the flavors, textures, and aromas of your food. By slowing down, you'll also be more likely to feel full and satisfied after a meal.

2. Pay Attention to Hunger and Fullness

Mindful eating also involves paying attention to your hunger and fullness levels. Before eating, take a moment to check in with yourself and ask whether you're really hungry, or just eating out of habit. And as you eat, be mindful of the sensations of hunger and fullness, and stop eating when you feel comfortably full.

3. Avoid Distractions

It's easy to become distracted while eating, but doing so can make it difficult to pay attention to what you're eating, and to your hunger and fullness levels. Try to eat your meals in a quiet, distraction-free environment, and focus your attention on the food and your body.

4. Be Grateful

Finally, being grateful for the food you're eating is an important part of mindful eating. Whether you take a moment to say grace, or simply reflect on the many people and resources that went into bringing your meal to your table, taking the time to appreciate your food will help you eat more mindfully and with greater intention.

By incorporating mindfulness into your eating and drinking, you'll be able to cultivate a deeper awareness of your body and your food and enjoy your meals with greater focus and intention.

C. Mindful Movement and Exercise

Physical activity is an important aspect of overall health and well-being, and practicing mindfulness during exercise can enhance the benefits even further. Here are some tips for incorporating mindfulness into your movement and exercise:

1. Focus on the Present Moment

One of the main benefits of mindful movement is that it helps you focus your attention on the present moment. Instead of letting your mind wander, try to focus on the sensations of your body as you move, and pay attention to your breath. This can help you feel more connected to your body and to the physical experience of exercise.

2. Start Slow

When starting a mindful movement practice, it's important to start slow and gentle. Focus on moving with ease and comfort, and avoid pushing yourself too hard or trying to do too much too soon. This will help you avoid injury and increase the likelihood of developing a regular practice.

3. Vary Your Practice

To avoid boredom and keep your mindfulness practice fresh, it's a good idea to vary your movements and exercises. This might mean trying new forms of physical activity, like yoga, tai chi, or dance, or simply changing the way you move.

4. Incorporate Breathing Exercises

Breathing exercises are an important aspect of many mindfulness practices and can be especially beneficial during movement and exercise. Incorporating deep, slow breaths into your movement practice can help you focus your attention, reduce stress, and increase oxygenation to your muscles.

By incorporating mindfulness into your movement and exercise, you'll be able to cultivate a deeper awareness of your body, reduce stress and anxiety, and enhance your physical and mental well-being.

D. Mindful Communication and Relationships

Mindfulness can also have a profound impact on our relationships with others. By becoming more aware of our thoughts, feelings, and behaviors, we can improve the quality of our interactions with others and deepen our connections. Here are some tips for incorporating mindfulness into your communication and relationships:

1. Listen Mindfully

One of the key components of mindful communication is paying attention to what the other person is saying. This means really listening, without judgment or distraction, to what they have to say. This can help build trust and respect, and deepen your understanding of the other person.

2. Speak Mindfully

In addition to listening mindfully, it's also important to be mindful in how you speak to others. This means avoiding reactive or defensive behavior, and instead speaking from a place of compassion and understanding. This can help improve the quality of your interactions and reduce conflict.

3. Practice Self-Reflection

Before engaging in communication with others, take a moment to reflect on your own thoughts and feelings. This can help you approach the conversation with greater awareness and empathy, and can also help you avoid knee-jerk reactions or negative behaviors.

4. Cultivate Empathy

Empathy is the ability to understand and share the feelings of others. By cultivating empathy, you can improve your relationships and increase the quality of your interactions. To develop empathy, try to imagine what it would be like to be in the other person's shoes, and approach each interaction with a compassionate and understanding attitude.

By incorporating mindfulness into your communication and relationships, you'll be able to build stronger connections with others, improve the quality of your interactions, and reduce conflict and stress.

VI. Advanced Mindfulness and Meditation Techniques

As you progress in your mindfulness and meditation practice, you may want to explore more advanced techniques to deepen your understanding and experience. Here are a few techniques you can try:

1. Loving-Kindness Meditation

Loving-kindness meditation is a practice of sending love, compassion, and well-wishes to others. This meditation can help cultivate compassion and empathy, and can also help reduce feelings of stress and anxiety. To practice loving-kindness meditation, start by focusing on yourself and generating feelings of love and kindness. Then, imagine sending these feelings to loved ones, friends, and eventually to all beings.

2. Body Scan Meditation

Body scan meditation involves lying down and focusing your attention on each part of your body, from the top of your head to the tips of your toes. This meditation can help you become more aware of physical sensations and release tension in the body.

3. Chakra Meditation

Chakra meditation involves focusing your attention on each of the seven chakras, or energy centers, in the body. This meditation can help balance the flow of energy in the body, improve physical and emotional well-being, and deepen your spiritual connection.

4. Mantra Meditation

Mantra meditation involves repeating a word or phrase, either out loud or silently, to calm the mind and focus attention. This meditation can help reduce stress and anxiety, and can also help improve focus and concentration.

These advanced mindfulness and meditation techniques can help deepen your practice and provide new avenues for exploration. However, it's important to remember that there's no right or wrong way to meditate, and what works best for you will depend on your personal preferences and needs.

By incorporating these advanced techniques into your practice, you can deepen your understanding of mindfulness and meditation, and reap the benefits of these powerful practices.

A. Mindful Breathing and Body Scanning

M indful breathing and body scanning are two simple yet powerful techniques that can help deepen your mindfulness and meditation practice.

Mindful Breathing: This technique involves focusing your attention on the sensation of breathing, counting each inhales and exhale, and noticing any thoughts or distractions that arise. Mindful breathing can help calm the mind, reduce stress and anxiety, and improve focus and concentration. To practice mindful breathing, find a comfortable seat, close your eyes, and simply pay attention to your breath.

Body Scanning: This technique involves lying down and focusing your attention on each part of your body, from the top of your head to the tips of your toes. Body scanning can help you become more aware of physical sensations, release tension in the body, and reduce stress and anxiety. To practice body scanning, find a comfortable place to lie down, close your eyes, and focus on one body part at a time, noticing any sensations and allowing them to pass.

These techniques are great starting points for those who are new to mindfulness and meditation, but they can also be practiced by those who are more experienced to deepen their practice. By incorporating mindful breathing and body scanning into your daily routine, you can cultivate a deeper sense of calm and peace in your life.

B. Loving-Kindness Meditation

Loving-kindness meditation, also known as metta meditation, is a powerful technique that can help cultivate feelings of love, compassion, and kindness towards yourself and others. This type of meditation involves repeating a series of phrases or affirmations, directed first towards yourself, then towards loved ones, neutral people, difficult people, and finally, all beings everywhere.

The purpose of this meditation is to help you overcome negative emotions such as anger, hatred, and jealousy, and to replace them with positive emotions such as love, compassion, and kindness. Practicing loving-kindness meditation can help you develop a more positive outlook on life, build stronger relationships with others, and increase your overall well-being.

To practice loving-kindness meditation, find a quiet place to sit or lie down, close your eyes, and repeat the following phrases or affirmations, focusing on each person or group as you say them:

- May I be happy.
- May I be healthy.
- May I be safe.
- May I live with ease.

Next, direct these phrases or affirmations toward a loved one, such as a partner or family member:

- May (loved one's name) be happy.
- May (loved one's name) be healthy.
- May (loved one's name) be safe.
- May (loved one's name) live with ease.

Continue the meditation by directing the phrases or affirmations towards neutral people, difficult people, and finally, all beings everywhere. As you practice this meditation, try to visualize each person or group surrounded by love and light, and imagine them experiencing the same positive emotions that you would like for yourself.

Loving-kindness meditation can be a challenging practice at first, but with regular practice, it can help you develop a more positive and compassionate outlook on life.

C. Chakra Meditation

Chakra meditation is a type of meditation that is centered around the seven energy centers, or chakras, in the body. These chakras are believed to be points of energy that run along the spine and control various aspects of physical, emotional, and spiritual well-being.

In chakra meditation, the practitioner focuses their attention on each chakra one by one, working to balance and harmonize the energy in each chakra. This can be done by visualizing a specific color and symbol associated with each chakra and reciting affirmations or mantras that are related to that chakra.

The seven chakras are:

1. Root chakra (Muladhara) - located at the base of the spine and associated with the color red, this chakra is related to stability, grounding, and a sense of belonging.
2. Sacral chakra (Svadhisthana) - located just below the navel

and associated with the color orange, this chakra is related to emotions, sexuality, and creativity.

3. Solar Plexus chakra (Manipura) - located in the stomach area and associated with the color yellow, this chakra is related to personal power, self-confidence, and self-esteem.
4. Heart chakra (Anahata) - located in the chest area and associated with the color green, this chakra is related to love, compassion, and connection to others.
5. Throat chakra (Vishuddha) - located in the throat area and associated with the color blue, this chakra is related to communication, self-expression, and authenticity.
6. Third Eye Chakra (Ajna) - located in the forehead area and associated with the color indigo, this chakra is related to intuition, perception, and inner wisdom.
7. Crown chakra (Sahaswara) - located at the top of the head and associated with the color violet, this chakra is related to spiritual connection and enlightenment.

Chakra meditation can help to improve physical, emotional, and mental health, increase self-awareness and foster spiritual growth. It can be a powerful tool for personal transformation and can help individuals to tap into their own inner wisdom and find a deeper sense of peace and contentment.

Muladhara
root chakra

Svadhishthana
sacral chakra

Manipura
solar chakra

Anahata
heart chakra

Vishuddha
throat chakra

Ajna
third chakra

Sahasrara
crown chakra

D. Mantra Meditation

Mantra meditation is a technique that involves repeating a sound or phrase, known as a mantra, in order to still the mind and achieve a state of relaxation and inner peace. This form of meditation is often used as a tool for stress relief and to cultivate a deeper connection to the self.

To practice mantra meditation, find a quiet and comfortable place to sit. Close your eyes and take a few deep breaths to relax your body and calm your mind. Choose a mantra that resonates with you – this could be a word or phrase in any language, a sound, or even a single syllable. Repeat the mantra silently or out loud, focusing your attention on the sound and allowing any thoughts or distractions to drift away.

It's important to approach mantra meditation with an open mind and a spirit of experimentation. There is no right or wrong way to do it, and you may find that you naturally gravitate towards different mantras at different times in your life. Some people choose to use prayer beads, to help them keep track of their repetitions and stay focused.

Mantra meditation can help to quiet the mind, reduce stress and anxiety, and improve overall mental clarity and focus. It can also be a tool for personal growth and spiritual exploration, helping you to connect with a deeper sense of meaning and purpose. With regular practice, you may find that your mantra becomes a source of comfort and peace, helping you to navigate life's challenges with greater ease.

VII. Conclusion

In conclusion, mindfulness and meditation are powerful tools for improving our mental, emotional, and physical well-being. Throughout this book, we have explored the definition and benefits of mindfulness, how to get started with simple techniques, how to incorporate mindfulness and meditation into daily life, and advanced practices such as chakra meditation and mantra meditation.

By taking the time to practice mindfulness and meditation regularly, you can experience reduced stress and anxiety, improved focus and productivity, deeper connections in relationships, and a greater sense of peace and inner calm.

Remember that mindfulness and meditation are ongoing practices, and like any skill, the more you put in, the more you will get out. So be patient with yourself and keep exploring the many different aspects of mindfulness and meditation, finding what works best for you.

We hope that this book has provided you with valuable information and inspiration to help you start or deepen your mindfulness and meditation practice. May you continue on your journey of self-discovery, growth, and well-being.

A. Summary of Key Points

The key points covered in the book include:

1. The definition of mindfulness and the science behind it, including how it has been shown to reduce stress and anxiety.
2. Simple mindfulness techniques for beginners, including how to improve focus and productivity using mindfulness.
3. Tips for overcoming obstacles to successful mindfulness practice and getting started with meditation, including different types of meditation and how to create a daily practice.
4. Incorporating mindfulness and meditation into daily life, including mindful eating, drinking, movement and exercise, and communication and relationships.
5. Advanced mindfulness and meditation techniques, such as mindful breathing and body

scanning, loving-kindness meditation, chakra meditation, and mantra meditation.

These points provide a comprehensive overview of mindfulness and meditation and offer practical guidance for readers looking to deepen their understanding and start their own practice.

B. Reflections on the Journey Ahead

As you conclude your exploration of mindfulness and meditation through this book, it's important to reflect on your own experiences with these practices. This can help you solidify your understanding of the benefits and techniques, and provide you with a framework for continued growth and development in the future.

Take some time to answer the following questions:

1. What were your initial thoughts and feelings about mindfulness and meditation?
2. Have your views changed after reading this book and practicing mindfulness and meditation?
3. What are some of the biggest benefits you have experienced through these practices?
4. What challenges have you encountered and how have you overcome them?
5. What do you hope to achieve through your continued

practice of mindfulness and meditation?

It can be helpful to write down your answers to these questions in a journal so that you can reflect on your growth and progress over time. Remember, this is a journey and not a destination, and it's important to be patient with yourself and celebrate your successes along the way.

By reflecting on your experiences with mindfulness and meditation, you can gain a deeper understanding of these practices and how they can help you to live a more fulfilling life. With this understanding and continued practice, you can develop a powerful toolkit for managing stress, improving your focus and productivity, and enhancing your relationships and overall well-being.

C. Final Thoughts

As we come to the end of this book, we hope that you have gained a deeper understanding of mindfulness and meditation and how you can incorporate these practices into your daily life. We have covered a lot of ground in this book, from the definition of mindfulness to the various techniques used to deepen our practice.

In this section, we would like to summarize the key points that we have covered and offer some reflections on the journey ahead.

Summary of Key Points:

- Mindfulness is a mental state achieved by focusing one's awareness on the present moment, while calmly acknowledging and accepting one's feelings, thoughts, and bodily sensations.
- The science behind mindfulness has shown that practicing

mindfulness can have a positive impact on our mental and physical well-being, reducing stress and anxiety, improving focus and productivity, and enhancing our relationships.
- There are various mindfulness and meditation techniques that can be used to deepen our practice, including mindful breathing, body scanning, loving-kindness meditation, chakra meditation, and mantra meditation.

Reflections on the Journey Ahead:

We encourage you to reflect on your own experiences with mindfulness and meditation. What were your initial thoughts and feelings about these practices? How have they impacted your life so far? How can you continue to grow and develop your practice?

Mindfulness and meditation are lifelong journeys and every moment of practice is valuable. Remember that there is no right or wrong way to practice and that it is a personal and unique experience for each person.

Personal Stories:

We would also like to share some personal experiences that we have had with mindfulness and meditation. For example, one of us found that practicing mindfulness helped to reduce stress and anxiety, while another found that it improved focus and productivity.

Final Thoughts:

In conclusion, we hope that this book has been a valuable resource for you and that you have gained a deeper understanding of the power of mindfulness and meditation. We wish you all the best on your journey ahead and hope that you continue to find joy and peace in your practice.

About the Author

Mind Muse is a meditation and mindfulness expert, who has dedicated their lives to exploring the many benefits of mindfulness and meditation. With a background in psychology and mindfulness studies, Mind Muse has a deep understanding of the mind and the power of mindfulness to improve our lives. Over the years, Mindful Muse has honed their craft through years of practice and study, becoming a well-respected teacher, speaker, and author in the mindfulness community. Their teachings focus on the practical application of mindfulness, helping individuals to cultivate a deeper awareness of themselves, others, and the world around them. Whether through books, workshops, or online courses, Mind Muse is dedicated to sharing their knowledge and helping others to find peace, happiness, and fulfillment through mindfulness and meditation.

Mindful Meditation

"Mindful Meditation" is an insightful guide to unlocking the power of mindfulness and meditation for a more fulfilling and purposeful life. Filled with practical tips, easy-to-follow exercises, and inspiring stories, this book will show you how to cultivate mindfulness in every aspect of your life, from relationships to work and beyond. Whether you're a complete beginner or an experienced practitioner, "Mindful Meditation" is the ultimate companion on your journey to inner peace, clarity, and happiness.